Lyric Journal:
Songwriter's Notebook

ISBN-13: 978-1505622218
ISBN-10: 1505622212

This Journal Belongs

to

____

Song Title:____________________
Inspiration:

Lyrics:

Music:

Song Title:
Inspiration:

Lyrics:

Music:

Song Title:________________________

Inspiration:

Lyrics:

Music:

Song Title:______________________
Inspiration:

Lyrics:

Music:

Song Title:

Inspiration:

Lyrics:

Music:

Song Title:________________________

Inspiration:

Lyrics:

Music:

Song Title:____________________
Inspiration:

Lyrics:

Music:

Song Title:____________________

Inspiration:

Lyrics:

Music:

Song Title:____________________
Inspiration:

Lyrics:

Music:

Song Title:____________________

Inspiration:

Lyrics:

Music:

Song Title:________________________

Inspiration:

____

____

____

Lyrics:

Music:

Song Title:____________________

Inspiration:

Lyrics:

Music:

Song Title:________________________
Inspiration:

Lyrics:

Music:

Song Title:____________________
Inspiration:

Lyrics:

Music:

Song Title:________________________

Inspiration:

Lyrics:

Music:

Song Title:________________________
Inspiration:

Lyrics:

Music:

Song Title: ______________________

Inspiration:

Lyrics:

Music:

Song Title:________________________

Inspiration:

Lyrics:

Music:

Song Title:____________________
Inspiration:

Lyrics:

Music:

Song Title:______________________
Inspiration:

Lyrics:

Music:

Song Title:____________________

Inspiration:

Lyrics:

Music:

Song Title:

Inspiration:

Lyrics:

Music:

Song Title:

Inspiration:

Lyrics:

Music:

Song Title:________________________
Inspiration:

____

____

____

Lyrics:

Music:

Song Title:____________________

Inspiration:

Lyrics:

Music:

Song Title:____________________

Inspiration:

Lyrics:

Music:

Song Title:____________________
Inspiration:

Lyrics:

Music:

Song Title:______________________

Inspiration:

Lyrics:

Music:

Song Title:________________________

Inspiration:

Lyrics:

Music:

Song Title:____________________

Inspiration:

Lyrics:

Music:

Lyric Journal

58242327R00058

Made in the USA
Lexington, KY
06 December 2016